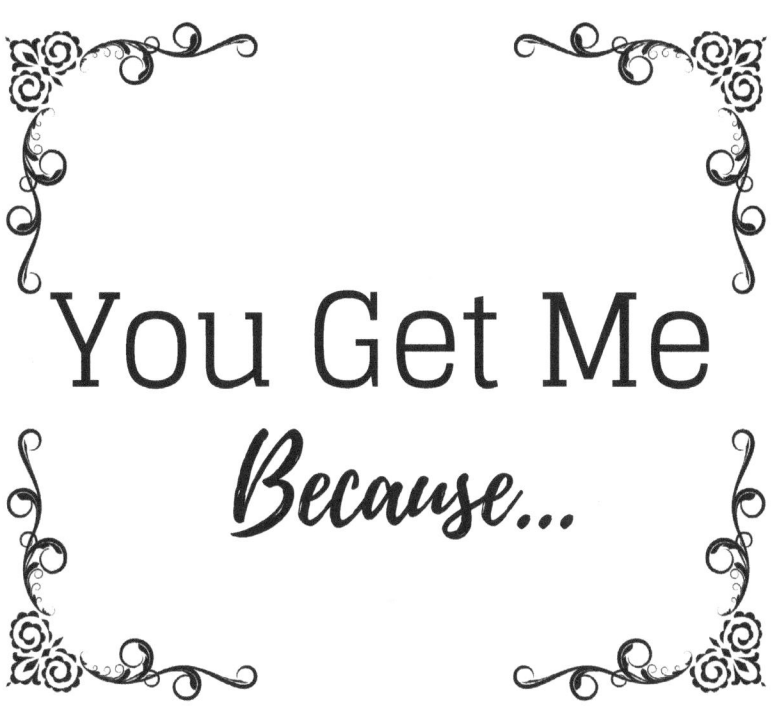

You Get Me
Because...

Our Daily Reflections

ISBN- 978-0-9769594-8-9

PUBLISHED BY:
CASTALIA MEDIA
PRINTED IN THE UNITED STATES OF
AMERICA

Get Your FREE Goodies because...

Jim writes...

There is a lot of cool stuff for couples!

Download your FREE Goodies at:
http://www.YouGetMeBecause/Goodies

Debra writes...

You and your partner will really enjoy the goodies!

Besides, it's FREE so why not.

This journal belongs to...

You get me
because...

I get goosebumps
when I think about how you...

What I remember most about the day we met is...

You're perfect for me because...

I acknowledge you for...

You make me laugh when you...

I admire you for your...

When I brag about you, I say...

Our most romantic moment was...

Thank you for supporting me on...

My favorite place to be with you is…

I appreciate you for...

My ideal day with you would be...

A life lesson I've learned from you is...

I knew I was in love
with you when...

I am grateful for your...

I like the way you...

When we are away from each other, what I miss most about you is...

I'm a better person when I'm around you because...

The quirkiest thing I love about you is...

If I could take you anywhere, it would be...

If our relationship were a song or a movie, it would be called...

I feel close to you when we...

I like when you...

I feel most supported by you when...

One of my favorite things
we do together is...

We make a good team because...

With you in my life,
a new possibility is...

If we only had one day left,
I would want to ...

The best part of our day together is…

I knew you were the
one for me when...

I am looking forward to
this year with you because...

What I remember most about our first kiss is...

One of your greatest strengths is…

Your best advice to me was...

You make me a better person when you...

The best gift you've given me is...

I love empowering you to…

A dream vacation
with you would be...

You have taught me how to...

Our most epic
moment together was...

I feel loved when you...

You help me through tough times when you...

What I respect most about you is...

I get butterflies when you...

A quality that I really admire about you is...

I am grateful for your...

You bring out the best in me because...

One of your greatest talents is your...

What I have learned about life and love from you is...

I am proud of you for...

You stopped me in my tracks when you...

Time flies with you when...

I'd like our next adventure to be...

I have a crush on you because...

You had me at...

One of the most important values we share is...

What I remember most about the first time I saw you is...

You're a good partner because...

You have my back when…

The sexiest thing about you is...

You make me smile when you...

I love you for...

My top three memories of us are...

When we are old, I hope we still...

You turn me on when you...

What I remember most about falling in love with you is...

You are my hero because…

I love when you wear...

Our best road trip was when we...

I'll never forget the time we...

One of the things I most value about our relationship is...

I promise you...

I'm happiest when we...

The best compliment
you've given me is...

If we were snowed in together I would want to...

I declare who I will be for you is...

I love that we share...

I feel bulletproof when you...

A little thing you do that I love is...

A perfect date night
with you would be...

If you had a superpower it would be...

My life is better with you in it because...

If I could only give you
one gift it would be...

The three adjectives I'd use to describe you are...

One wish I have for you is...

My biggest hope & dream for you is...

Who you are for me is...

I feel safe with you because...

You're my best friend because...

You're awesome because...

You inspire me to...

You have THE best...

You're a badass when...

My intention for us is to...

You're adorable when you...

I cherish your...

It is *SO* much fun when we…

I want us to create...

I respect you for...

You take my breath away when...

You're like a big kid when you...

When we are together I feel...

A sacrifice you make for us that I really appreciate is...

Psst,...

About the Authors...

I am dedicated to bringing fun, engaging, educational and inspiring books to both children and adults.

I am committed to appreciating beauty in everyday life and to encouraging loving, joyful relationships,.

Please Leave a Review Because...

Jim writes...

Your reviews will help others decide if the book is right for them. As an independent author, the success of this book depends, in large part, on Amazon reviews. Thank you.

Debra writes...

Reviews play a very important role in determining the success of a book. It would mean a lot to Jim and I if you could leave us a review. Thanks.

Get Your FREE Goodies...

Jim writes...

There are lots of fun and engaging activities for couples so don't forget to claim yours now.

Download your FREE Goodies at:
http://www.YouGetMeBecause/Goodies

Debra writes...

It's FREE so why not? Besides, you deserve it!

www.ingramcontent.com/pod-product-compliance
Lightning Source LLC
Chambersburg PA
CBHW060510280326
41933CB00014B/2911

* 9 7 8 0 9 7 6 9 5 9 4 8 9 *